We who choose to surround ourselves with lives even more temporary than our own
live within a fragile circle, easily and often breached. Yet, still we would live no other way."

Irving Townsend

Simple Things

by Alan Cunningham

When did I last hold you
Or did I let time slip away,
And isn't it the simple things
That make life beautiful day by day.

Alan Holding CC

Fragile Tears

Stories & Guidance for Youth on the Passing Away
of
Beloved Animal Companions

Compiled by Alan Blain Cunningham, PhD, DVM, MD

Fragile Tears: Stories & Guidance for Youth on the Passing Away of Beloved Animal Companions.

Compiled by Alan Blain Cunningham, PhD, DVM, MD

Publisher's Cataloging-in-Publication Data
Cunningham, Alan Blain.
 Fragile Tears: Stories & Guidance for Youth on the Passing Away of Beloved Animal Companions / Alan Blain Cunningham. – 1st ed.
  p.cm

  ISBN: 1-888106-67-0

1. Pet Owners – Psychology. 2. Pets – Death – Psychological Aspects. 3. Bereavement – Psychological Aspects. 4. Grief. 5. Pets – United States – Anecdotes – Juvenile Literature. I. Title.

SF411.47.C374 2005   LC 2004117478
155.9'37 – dc21

The Best of State Awards were created to recognize outstanding individuals, organizations and businesses in Utah. Utah is a great place to live and work, and there is so much that is deserving of recognition.

Front Cover Art Chloe by Arianna Alexis
Chloe is one of Alan's Boston Terriers
Back Cover Art Alan Blain Cunningham
Cover Design Lea Taylor

This book was printed in the United States of America.

Agreka™ LLC
800 360-5284
www.agreka.com

Ascending to Heaven

Peace Rose

Dedication

This book is dedicated to the many children and youth who have been fortunate enough to have loved and lost an animal companion. Many consider the animal companion to be their first, best, and truest friend. And to some, the loss of an animal friend is their first exposure to death.

Appreciation is expressed to the contributors of Fragile Tears—the authors, artists, poets, songwriters, singers and musicians. A special thanks to Gary Stoddard for helping me to create the CD for this book. My love and gratitude is extended to Gary. He is a true friend. He radiates brilliant colors of generosity, talent, acceptance and joy!

Also I thank the many wonderful teachers that have taught me how to appreciate the glorious world and its wonders. From the delicate newborn animals, and scented flowers; to the great man made cathedrals and structures; and to the natural masterpieces of the waterfalls, mountains, and forests. Life, in all its simpleness and complexity, is beautiful and worth living. May we always appreciate, protect and preserve its universal sanctity and find peace with one another.

"Learning to love yourself is the most important thing to do. To share the love you give away and give some back to you. Open your heart and let everyone in and leave the door open wide. When you learn to love yourself is when you let yourself inside." Gary Stoddard

Contents

Illustrations

Introduction

Youth especially have a difficult time with the loss of a beloved animal companion. Because often times it is their first exposure to death, or the animal is their very first best friend. Grief over the loss of a beloved animal companion can be devastating and isolating. Many times society doesn't recognize or accept the depth of grief that people experience.

After the uncontrollable tears of sadness, we begin to heal, sometimes very slowly. Gradually, as we begin to heal, we remember our lost loved one with mixed emotions of grief and joy. And often times, without the slightest warning, we feel a delicate tear on our cheek. A fragile tear created mostly by love. May this book provide comfort and guidance to youth that have lost a beloved animal companion.

The complimentary CD, Fragile Tears, is also a compilation of music from various artists. It is meant to provide positive and reflective healing to the listener.

Sincerely, Alan Blain Cunningham

Fragile Tears

by Alan Cunningham

Fragile tears are symbolic of pure and innocent grief and joy. They too can be various colors and sizes, much like a rainbow, or rainbow tears. And although they often represent sadness, tears can also reflect brilliant colors of happiness.

Sometimes tears of sorrow can become too heavy for us to carry alone, and then we must allow others to help us. Like a dove in flight, others can lift our spirits and help carry our burdens away.

And if we are patient, and listen very carefully, we can hear the tears gently brush against each other in the pleasant sounds of the wind chimes, streams, birds, oceans, and nature all around. And then we are at peace and become healed.

Section 1

Tribute to a Best Friend

Tribute To A Best Friend

Author Unknown

Sunlight streams through window pane
unto a spot on the floor...
then I remember,
it's where you used to lie,
but now you are no more.
Our feet walk down a hall of carpet,
and muted echoes sound...
then I remember,
It's where your paws would joyously abound.
A voice is heard along the road,
and up beyond the hill,
then I remember it con't be yours...
your golden voice is still.
But I'll take that vacant spot of floor
and empty muted hall
and lay them with the absent voice
and unused dish along the wall.
I'll wrap these treasured memorials
in a blanket of my love
and keep them for my best friend
until we meet above.

The Fourth Day

by Martin Scot Kosins

If you ever love a dog, there are three days in your life you will always remember.

The first is a day, blessed with happiness, when you bring home your young new friend.

You may have spent weeks deciding on a breed. You may have asked numerous opinions of many vets, or done long research in finding a breeder.

Or, perhaps in a fleeting moment, you may have just chosen that silly looking mutt in a shelter – simply because something in its eyes reached your heart.

But when you bring that chosen pet home, and watch it explore, and claim its special place in your hall or front room – and when you feel it brush against you for the first time – it instills a feeling of pure love you will carry with you through the many years to come.

The second day will occur eight or nine or ten years later.

It will be a day like any other. Routine and unexceptional. But, for a surprising instant, you will look at your longtime friend and see age where you once saw youth.

You will see slow deliberate steps where you once saw energy.

And you will see sleep when you once saw activity.

So you will begin to adjust your friend's diet – and you may add a pill or two to her food.

And you may feel a growing fear deep within yourself, which bodes of a coming emptiness.

And you will feel this uneasy feeling, on and off, until the third day finally arrives.

And on this day – if your friend and God have not decided for you, then you will be faced with making a decision of your own – on behalf of your lifelong friend, and with the guidance of your own deepest Spirit.

But whichever way your friend eventually leaves you – you will feel as lone as a single star in the dark night.

If you are wise, you will let the tears flow as freely and as often as they must. And if you are typical, you will find that not many in your circle of family or friends will be able to understand your grief, or comfort you.

But if you are true to the love of the pet you cherished through the many joy-filled years, you may find that a soul – a bit smaller in size than your own – seems to walk with you, at times, during the lonely days to come.

And at moments when you least expect anything out of the ordinary to happen, you may feel something brush against your leg – very, very lightly.

And looking down at the place where your dear, perhaps dearest, friend used to lie – you will remember those three significant days.

The memory will most likely be painful, and leave an ache in your heart –

As time passes the ache will come and go as if it has a life of its own.

You will both reject it and embrace it, and it may confuse you.

If you reject it, it will depress you.

If you embrace it, it will deepen you.

Either way, it will still be an ache.

But there will be, I assure you, a fourth day when – along with the memory of your pet – and piercing through the heaviness in your heart – there will come a realization that belongs only to you.

It will be as unique and strong as our relationship with each animal we have loved, and lost.

This realization takes the form of a Living Love –

Like the heavenly scent of a rose that remains after the petals have wilted, this Love will remain and grow – and be there for us to remember.

It is a love we have earned.

It is the legacy our pets leave us when they go –

And it is a gift we may keep with us as long as we live.

It is a Love which is ours alone –

And until we ourselves leave, perhaps to join our Beloved Pets –

It is a Love we will always possess.

Martin Scot Kosins is the author of Maya's First Rose, published by Open Sky Books.

"The Fourth Day" originally appeared as the Foreword for *Pet Loss* by Nieburg and Fischer, published by Harper Perennial.

Published here with permission of Martin Scot Kosins.

Angel

by Alan Cunningham

My Boston Terrier, Pug, quietly left me six months ago. I deeply miss her still and probably always will. Daily I visit her grave in my yard and talk with her. Sometimes I shed a few tears. And I thank Pug for sharing her precious life with me for nearly eleven years.

In July, 2002, Pug was diagnosed with a blood clot in her right front leg. With aggressive anticoagulant therapy, daily bandage changes, and pain medications, we were able to restore circulation to her leg, although she lost her toes.

Selfishly I fought to restore Pug to health. When I removed the wraps from her leg and debrided the dead tissue, I could detect the pain in her eyes. Large, almond-shaped eyes that once danced with innocent mischievousness and happiness were now dulled with agony. Pug looked at me as if to say she had enough. But I refused to listen. I would not let her go. For nearly a month she patiently endured without complaint.

Since I am a veterinarian at a nighttime emergency clinic, I was able to take Pug to work with me and provide her medical care. One of my other dogs, C.C., who is also a Boston Terrier, accompanied me to work as well. Pug and C.C. were best friends. Pug was like a mother to C.C.

At the veterinary clinic I have my own bedroom to rest in when work is slow. Around five a.m. Pug awoke and gazed over the side of the bed.

"Are you okay, little girl?" I asked.

She just quietly peered over the side of the bed at her food and water dish.

I helped her down and she slowly drank water.

"Let's go outside to the bathroom, you two."

I carried Pug, and C.C. followed. Afterwards we returned to the bedroom. When I placed Pug on the bed, she began to breath laboriously and then suddenly collapsed. Before I could do anything Pug had passed away. She was now free from physical torment and had angel wings to fly.

I reflect back and realize that she graciously awoke one last time to say goodbye. At the time, I was devastated and heartbroken. Pug was my angel, my joy, and my strength.

"When Pug leaves, I will too," I had repeatedly announced to myself.

Aspen

If not for my other animals, dear friends, and family, I would have given up. I anguished over returning to work and being in the room and bed that Pug died in. How could I relive it?

"On the other hand," I thought, "the room has become almost sacred and inspirational to me."

I contemplated that upon returning to work I could either continue to grieve or I could utilize my energy in a more productive manner.

I pledged to remember the beautiful times with Pug and with unstoppable energy chose to share them with other people by writing her story as it intertwined with my life.

At night, when the clinic was quiet, I would record her memory. I felt Pug was with me, directing the thoughts while I wrote them on paper. In three weeks her remarkable story in *Sleeping With Angels* was completed.

Sadly, as a veterinarian, I witness too many animal deaths. And I recognize many pet owners experience extreme sorrow from the loss of a beloved animal companion. Tonight at work, for example, I euthanized an eight year old Keeshound with kidney failure. The single, elderly owner sobbed that she could not bear to watch her dear friend, Cleo, suffer. She decided, after the euthanasia, to have Cleo privately cremated and the ashes returned. "Please take good care of her," she wept.

"May I share something special with you?" I asked as I handed her a copy of my book. She eagerly looked at it and read out loud, "Sleeping With Angels." She then looked at me with a tearful smile and gently announced, "Now I know what we will have engraved on Cleo's epitaph – Cleo, Sleeping with Angels."

Not only did I deeply remorse over Pug's death, but so did C.C. Her youthful four-year-old face turned prematurely gray almost overnight. Instead of playfully passing the day with Pug as she used to she now laid sadly in the recliner chair that she and Pug once shared together.

Pug and C.C. used to good-naturedly compete for my affection. When Pug died, C.C. quietly stood back and allowed me to grieve privately while I held Pug. Little did I realize the pain that C.C. also experienced.

"She is grieving more than we realize," Mom announced.

Regretfully, in my own sorrow, I had forgotten C.C.

At night C.C. would stretch herself across my pillow and protectively push tightly against my head, while Aspen, my three-legged Black Labrador Retriever, comfortably slept at my feet.

"Goodnight, angels," I would whisper and then realize the absence of Pug. She used to cuddle snugly next to my stomach. As I started to cry, C.C. would immediately stand up and lick the tears from my face. Perhaps she was grieving as much for me as for the loss of Pug.

When I would leave home on my quest to visit the Wonders of the World, Pug would eagerly follow me to the door.

"I have to go by myself this time little girl, you need to stay home."

Dejectedly she would turn away from me and slowly retire to her chair. She made me feel extremely guilty without saying a word.

"I'll be back," I called to her as I left.

Mom informed me that Pug would seldom leave the sanctuary of her recliner chair when I was gone. She seemed to mourn my absence and would spend most of her time sleeping.

As a result, whenever I left for distant countries, I would phone home to talk with Pug. The sound of my voice seemed to cheer her up.

"How's my little girl? Are you being good?"

According to mom, Pug would twist her head, perk up her ears, and open her eyes with alert attentiveness as I talked with her.

Wherever I went — China, New Zealand, Australia, Turkey, Jordan, Zimbabwe, Peru, India, Brazil, Italy — anyplace in the world, my first priority was to call home and talk to Pug after I arrived.

Pug, how I yearn to call you again. But I can only imagine the brightness in your eyes and the eagerness in your body as you intently listen to my voice.

Now you have left me and I eagerly await to hear from you. And I realize that in your own way you are sending me daily greetings.

I received your wonderful Christmas gift. She was a bundle of brown and white fur only weighing one pound and nine ounces. The crested fur on her head curled inwards like a chrysanthemum. I have long admired the attentive, large eyes of Shih Tzu dogs. Their curious, thoughtful glances seem to look deep into the heart of your soul.

Forgive me, Pug, but I don't understand why you sent her to me in such a tattered package. She entered the world experiencing much the same physical pain and torment that you left behind. Perhaps you want me to understand that everything valuable is worth fighting for.

She arrived at the emergency clinic the morning after Christmas, only six weeks old. Her owner puzzled over the constant, severe pain she was enduring. Not only was she constantly painful, she was also blind. Unable to pay for necessary treatment of a pup with an uncertain future, and yet unwilling to euthanize the poor little soul, the owner relinquished her to the hospital.

Pug, can you imagine the fear the delicate little pup must have felt experiencing a dark world full of pain. When I arrived at work that night and saw her and heard of her plight, I immediately asked the charge veterinarian if I could have her. "Yes," he returned. "Now try and figure out why she is so painful."

Even with pain medications the fragile pup moaned in severe agony. The radiographs showed nothing abnormal. I debated that euthanasia would be the kindest thing for her. While I quietly and sadly watched her suffer a thought came to me. Had they considered spinal meningitis? Quickly I researched the disease and realized that it was worth a try. It may take several days or even weeks but she could recover. After all, she was my responsibility now and she deserved a fighting chance. Pug, somehow I felt you were helping me with this battle.

I took the tiny creature home. Every four hours I tube fed the tiny pup. She received pain medications and antibiotics as needed. Unfortunately over the next several days she remained the same.

One more day, I bargained, then I will mercifully euthanize her. That night, for a short while, she seemed to be more quiet and peaceful. I feared that she had died. But when I felt for her, I discovered that she had moved from her bed and nestled next to my stomach. At first I thought you had returned, Pug. Then I realized that the little thing must be getting better.

The tiny bundle of joy and enthusiasm is now twelve weeks old and full of puppy freedom. She and C.C. cavort together like you and C.C. once did. Her ulcerated eyes are better and she now looks at me with a turned head and intent stare much as you used to.

Aspen has even fallen in love with her, or at least she patiently tolerates her. The little girl loves to play with Aspen's tail, while Aspen just lays there with a grin on her face.

I've introduced her to the big boys – Brownie, Golden, and Moose. But since she is only a four pound morsel, I will allow some more time before integrating her with them. And although she is the smallest of all my family of dogs, she barks out the loudest orders!

One of her favorite activities is to steal mom's shoes and hide them in the bedroom. By the way, mom visits your grave every day and talks with you. She tells me, "I had a good talk with Pug today, and she is doing fine."

You know how much I miss you, Pug. You are always in my heart. I trust you and Dad are enjoying each other, spending time together in the fragrant meadows.

Please prepare a place for Aspen as I fear her time on earth is nearing to an end. With her one missing leg, and debilitating arthritis, I have to carry her most of the time now.

Pug, thanks for giving me the tiny package of Christmas joy. She does so many things that remind me of you. Because of her petite flat nose she snores at night, only not as loudly as you did. You know how much I love flat-nosed dogs. With her inquisitive nature she has discovered your secret hiding place underneath the living room couch. She also loves to cuddle up next to my stomach as you used to. And I still feel like I'm sleeping with angels.

Do you know how refreshing it is to occasionally view the world through a puppy's eyes? I'm sure you do. That is why you sent her to me – to remove me from the grief of your loss. She has become a precious gift. Thank you Pug.

And one last thing, my beloved. I have chosen a name for her. Her name is Angel.

Angel

22

Beau

by Laura Taylor

I'll share a story I wrote years ago. I was thirteen years old and we had just moved to Kansas City, leaving all my friends behind. What follows is that story. . .

Mom suggests we take a drive and soon we are in unfamiliar territory. Almost out of town, the car bounces over deep ruts.

A long one-story building sits in the middle of nowhere. *What is this place?*

Breathing frosty puffs into the frigid air, we pull open the heavy door. Hundreds of dogs are barking. Cages line a maze of corridors.

"Are we going to get a dog!" I ask, my heart leaping with anticipation. My last dog had run away.

"You find the one you like best and, if he's small enough for our townhouse, we'll get him."

Slowly I walk down the long cement aisle. There are so many and all want homes so badly, someone to love and take care of them.

"Oh, Mom, I don't know which one. They're all begging." Little ones, big ones, even puppies. So many begging me, yelping louder and louder. Then I see him — a little Chihuahua mix huddled alone in a corner at the far end, quivering. I walk toward this last cage, set away from the others. The attendant says, "Trucker brought him in. Found him in the middle a nowhere, kicked half to death. Too damaged to make a good pet."

"I'll take him."

"Little girl, he's too screwed up. You know, emotional; too damaged to respond to anybody. Take one of them cute puppies back there."

"No, he's the one I want. Okay, Mom?" She smiles.

Shaking his head, the attendant unlocks the cage and hands me this terrified tiny, blonde creature. Crusty sores cover his little body and big patches of hair are missing. I cradle him in my arms and talk to him softly. I tell him I'll love him and take care of him and never, ever hurt him. He then proceeds to pee all over me.

Laura holding Beau

24

On the way home, Mom says, "Honey, he is the most pitiful looking creature I've ever seen in my life."

"I know, Mom, that's why I want him." At home I make him a terrific bed with a pillow and my best blanket. Mom leaves to buy him some food and treats. I stretch out on the floor and croon reassurances to this precious creature so damaged by cruelty.

"His name is Beauregard," I announce to Mom the next day.

"Has he come out of his bed yet?" she asks.

"No, but he will soon. He's not shaking as bad, and he finally ate a few bites. You just watch. I'll have him well in no time."

And so Beau comes into my life. I love him. And he loves me. Ever so slowly, he responds to my love and tender care. After a week he lets me give him a bath with my best shampoo and conditioner.

But, as the weeks pass, I finally realize he really is permanently damaged. No question about it. He has some quirks that just aren't normal. He's entitled, I guess, after getting kicked until he's almost dead. But we belong together. We're a team.

Beau went with me everywhere. He was afraid to go down the stairs, but I would go down a couple of stairs and patiently wait for him to follow. Finally he was flying down the stairs with me.

Whenever I was sad or crying Beau would slowly creep over to me to snuggle and lick my face until I laughed.

Four years later, after moves to two more new cities because of my mom's company transferring her, we realized Beau simply could not handle all the commotion of so many changes. Beau bared his teeth at me, and I felt like a stranger. Over the next month, we watched him go crazy. Mom and I looked at each other and knew what we had to do. We fought back tears. We had done everything in the world for him; but it wasn't enough. Beau had given all he had to give.

"Can you do it?" I whispered to Mom.

I lay in bed that night staring at the ceiling, tears soaking my pillow. Awakening to silence the next morning, I dash from room to room, searching frantically for Beau. He is not there.

Beau had been my closest friend, my dear companion. I'll never forget Beau. And I know he swiftly traveled to a better place where one day we'll be reunited.

At long last, he is healed.

Heart Prints

Dolly

Author Unknown

A farmer had some puppies he needed to sell. He painted a sign advertising the pups and set about nailing it to a post on the edge of his yard.

As he was driving the last nail into the post, he felt a tug on his overalls. He looked down into the eyes of a little boy.

Mister, "he said, "I want to buy one of your puppies."

"Well," said the farmer, as he rubbed the sweat off the back of his neck, "these puppies come from fine parents and cost a good deal of money."

The boy dropped his head for a moment. Then reaching deep into his pocket, he pulled out a handful of change and held it up to the farmer. "I've got thirty-nine cents. Is that enough to take a look?"

"Sure," said the farmer.

And with that he let out a whistle, "Here, Dolly!" he called. Out from the doghouse and down the ramp ran Dolly followed by four little balls of fur.

The little boy pressed his face against the chain link fence. His eyes danced with delight. As the dogs made their way to the fence, the little boy noticed something else stirring inside the doghouse. Slowly another little ball appeared; this one noticeably smaller. Down the ramp it slid. Then in a somewhat awkward manner the little pup began hobbling toward the others, doing its best to catch up.

"I want that one," the little boy said, pointing to the runt.

The farmer knelt down at the boy's side and said, "Son, you don't want that puppy. He will never be able to run and play with you like these other dogs would."

With that the little boy stepped back from the fence, reached down, and began rolling up one leg of his trousers. In doing so he revealed a steel brace running down both sides of his leg attaching itself to a specially made shoe.

Looking back up at the farmer, he said, "You see, sir, I don't run too well myself, and he will need someone who understands."

George

George, Our Pekingese

by Ann Shields

Dear Son,

I sit here as you come to me with tears in your eyes. You have just laid to rest a friend who has stood by you for twenty of your twenty-two years. For a few days you will remember him vividly. But then he will pass into the other special memories of your childhood as you go on to other pursuits and perhaps one day even replace him. You will never forget him entirely because he was your first pet.

He came to you with wagging tail and licking tongue when you were but a lad of two.

He asked no quota of anyone, except love, a pat on the back, and food when hungry. In return, he gave of himself many fold – unconditional love at its best.

When young, he was full of life – enjoying everything to the fullest and making you and others around him feel good just by his antics.

As you grew into a teenager and were out at night, he waited up for you – no matter if it was midnight from a date or earlier in the evening from church or school. He knew you would be home by ten p.m. and in some way he knew when it reached that time. He began his vigil then, which often included more pacing than even I did. His curfew was tougher than mine.

Each morning he would wait at the head of the stairs for you to turn on your light, then would go about his business, knowing all was right with his boy. At other times he would stop, not bothering you, but watching his special friend study or read, and be content just to be near.

When you left home, he kept up the ritual, not understanding why the light no longer shone nor his friend appear and why no one waited up for you at night.

Advancing years caught up with him, as it does with all of us, and he began walking slower, with a touch of arthritis in his legs. He was happy to spend his time lying against the heater.

His teeth were knocked out when his legs gave away and he tumbled down the basement stairs. Gradually his eyesight failed and his hearing went, but still he didn't complain, asking only for love, food, and a warm place to sleep. Then, having lost his perception, he began going in circles when attempting to move alone. And yet, he remained a faithful friend.

Now he has left us, but his memory will always be with us and his presence felt in our heart – a small black Pekingese with his distinctive white markings.

Just a dog, although a female, named George.

I Stood By Your Bed Last Night

Author Unknown

I stood by your bed last night, I came to have a peek. I could see that you were crying.
You found it hard to sleep. I whined to you softly as you brushed away a tear,
"It's me, I haven't left you, I'm well, I'm fine, I'm here."

I was close to you at breakfast, I watched you pour the tea. You were thinking of the
many times your hands reached down to me. I was with you at the shops today.
Your arms were getting sore. I longed to take your parcels, I wish I could do more.

I was with you at my grave today. You tend it with such care. I want to reassure you,
that I'm not lying there. I walked with you towards the house, as you fumbled for
your key. I gently put my paw on you, I smiled and said "It's me."

You looked so very tired, and sank into a chair. I tried so hard to let you know, that I
was standing there. It's possible for me to be so near you everyday. To say to you
with certainty, "I never went away."

You sat there very quietly, then smiled, I think you knew...in the stillness of that evening,
I was very close to you. The day is over...I smile and watch you yawning
and say "Goodnight, God bless, I'll see you in the morning."

And when the time is right for you to cross the brief divide, I'll rush across to greet you
and we'll stand, side by side. I have so many things to show you there is so much
for you to see. Be patient, live your journey out...then come home to be with me.

31

Henry & Dale

Henry, My Parrot

by Dale Layer

A sack of small birds captured in Sao Paulo, Brazil, was brought into town to sell.

Our son was a missionary in Brazil at the time and thought it would be a fitting gift for his parents when he returned to the states. He knew he would have access to the bird for six months before his return home, so he could satisfy the quarantine on birds being brought into the U.S.

Our son Dave is a character, and named the bird "Hemorrhoid" because he was a "pain in the rear." I'm sure the reason had to do with his care and the inconvenience in transferring him, and his registration during the six months before leaving. Needless to say, his arrival in the states was as "Henry," and his original name never surfaced again.

Henry was a small bird and the few words he had in his vocabulary were Portuguese, which is spoken in Brazil. He repeated the word "Loro" (meaning Bird) many times, but did pick up my wife Ruth's and my name Dale very quickly. The strange part was that Ruth's name was always in my voice and my name in her voice. This is natural when you think of it since they mimic not only the name but duplicate the sound of the voice, so Ruth was referred to in a low voice resembling mine.

Ruth took Henry to school during class time to the delight of her second grade children. Unfortunately, his tenure was short-lived since the rule of "speaking out of turn" was violated so many times that by lunch time he was expelled.

His other downfall at school was his bath in his water dish, which made one end of the schoolroom like a rain forest. In addition to attending school, he also went with us on church outings. He was a riot. The kids loved him and said he was one "fat" bird.

He also identified us by sounds of entry into the house – car engine noise and even our footsteps when we were out of sight. When hearing my car enter the driveway he would get excited and loudly call "Dale, Dale, Dale" for attention.

On returning from work I would spend time talking to him and doing his favorite things: Having his stomach stroked as he lay on his back with his feet in the air, or scratching the back of his neck while his head was tucked on his breast.

Our next door neighbors had three teenagers and many pets, and often cared for Henry when we were on vacation. On one occasion, however, Grandma volunteered to watch Henry while we were gone for a week. She lived alone and looked forward to his company and "chatter."

Unfortunately Henry died while we were gone and we were all devastated. We were told that it could have been from loneliness or from being over-indulged with grapes or other offerings. Whatever the reason, we came home to an empty, quiet cage.

We understand that parrots frequently live many years and had hoped that Henry would follow that trend. He was with us two years.

I was devastated and for months missed my excited greeting of "Dale, Dale, Dale," and play sessions with my "buddy." He was always cheerful when we were "down" and looked forward to our arrivals.

Henry was not just a pet, but an important part of our family.

Angel's Eyes

by Alan Cunningham

In Angel's eyes I see
What love is meant to be
She lightens up my life
She gives me sight to see

Softly, softly, softly
She dances at my feet
Gently, gently, gently
On angels wings she goes

Her coat of white
Her eyes of brown
Her upturned nose
Without a frown

Although her eyes
Will see no light
No rainbow colors
Of pure delight

Softly, softly, softly
She dances at my feet
Gently, gently, gently
On angels wings she goes

In Angel's eyes I see
What love is meant to be
She lightens up my life
She gives me sight to see
She gives me sight to see

Arianna
© Alexis
2004

Ole Blue

Ole Blue: A Story for KD Lawrence

by Diane Hunter

"Squawk, squawk," Ole Blue said, as he sat on Grandma Di's porch.

"What a beauty," Grandma Di said. "What will you eat, Ole Blue?"

"Squawk, squawk," again he said.

Grandma Di went to the cupboard and got a pickle and placed it in the little bird dish.

"Squawk, squawk," said Ole Blue.

Grandma Di said, "Oh my, the pickle won't do!" She went to the cupboard and soon placed a cookie in the dish.

"Squawk, Squawk," said Ole Blue. "That won't do. What in the world is wrong with you?" To the cupboard again, just for Ole Blue. She pulled out a carrot and placed it in the tiny dish.

"Squawk, Squawk," said Ole Blue. A carrot won't do, my beak is too small." What in the world is wrong with you?"

Old Grandma ran to the fridge and put some ice cream in the tiny dish.

"Squawk, squawk," said Ole Blue. "That won't do. The ice cream will melt. What in the world is wrong with you? I eat the same things as elephants do."

To the store ran Grandma Di as fast as she could. She bought a banana. She raced home and placed it in the tiny dish.

"Squawk, squawk," said Ole Blue. "That won't do. But the monkeys will love it at the zoo. What in the world is wrong with you?"

Grandma Di took a bucket to the cupboard and filled it with fruits and vegetables. She placed the bucket near the little dish on the porch.

"Squawk, squawk," said Ole Blue. "That won't do. But the lions will love it at the zoo. What in the world is wrong with you? I eat the same things that elephants do."

"What shall we do?" Grandma Di said in dismay. "Elephants do sometimes eat hay. But I have no hay. I'll try again another day."

"Squawk, squawk," said Ole Blue.

"Nuts to you!" said Grandma Di.

Ole Blue said, "Squawk, squawk. That's just what you SHOULD do! What in the world is wrong with you?"

"Here's a peanut, you silly old bird," said Grandma Di. "But how will you eat it? I don't care," said Grandma Di. "You probably won't like it anyway."

"Squawk, squawk," said Ole Blue. "The peanut will do! There's NOTHING at all that is wrong with you."

Jessie

Jessie Saves the Day

by Wes Treptow

I find myself telling this story from time to time.

Even though it happened over half my lifetime ago, I tell it both with a sense of pride and a small bit of sorrow for the dog long gone, whom I grew up with. Most people think I exaggerate when I tell it, but I guarantee that everything I'm about to tell you is absolutely true.

I suppose I should tell a little about my dog Jessie, and what made her the dog she was. The first time I saw her was at the animal shelter. The thing that stood out about her was, as the other dogs barked and howled and jumped around in their kennels, she sat quietly at her gate watching with great interest, not making a sound.

The single mom and two young sons were struck by her demeanor. My mother opened the kennel door and the puppy swaggered out to my brother and me, happily wagging her tail and licking our hands.

Mom read the tag on the door, "sex: female." It was my mother's stipulation that she be, well, a she. "Name: Boo-Boo."

"I think we're going to have to change that name."

Jessie, as my brother and I named her, grew to be a loyal friend who was willing to come to our defense at the first sign of trouble. Our mother never worried about us when Jessie was along.

We lived near a ravine called Dimple Dell, an equestrian park in Sandy, Utah, where my brother and I spent most of our summers hiking and doing whatever else two young teenage boys could think to do.

One day we hiked to a place in the park where it had been filled in to put a main road through. Now there were two ways to get to the other side. One was to walk through the huge culvert, which allowed the creek to pass under the road. This day that was not an option. It was a warm spring day and the culvert was deep with water, so we choose the other way, which was to hike to the top, across the road, and go back down the other side.

As we came out of the ravine, we saw three older guys, maybe late teens or early twenties. They had the classic look of people your mother warned you to stay away from.

They were nearby, each one with a big, mean-looking dog.

I'll never forget the dogs. The first of the three being what appeared to be a German Shepherd cross, the second having the unmistakable look of a Pit Bull, and the third and smallest of the three, a medium-sized brown mutt about the same size as Jessie.

My brother grabbed Jessie's collar tight. We didn't want any trouble with the dogs or the people. We tried to slip past unnoticed.

"Get em!" the guys shouted at their dogs as they turned them loose. My brother and I turned to run back down the trail, but Jessie jerked back, forced her head out of the collar, and faced down the three dogs.

The next minute or so seemed to last forever. On one side, the three dogs looking to kill something, anything. On the other side, Jessie willing to defend my brother and me at all costs.

Jessie stood unwavering. Her stance low and wide, her hackles raised, shoulders arched down and teeth bared. Her growl was so feral, remembering it still sends shivers down my spine.

The first dog, the Shepherd mix, made its move trying to get to my brother and me. Jessie waited until the Shepherd had separated itself from the other two dogs, then charged full force into it, sending it rolling several times. Then she jumped on top of the dog when it ended up on its back.

The Pit Bull jumped Jessie, grabbing the back of her neck. She twisted sharply, pulling it off her and to the ground by biting its shoulder. Jessie broke free just in time to intercept the third dog as it charged at her, knocking it off its feet and going for its throat.

Then the Shepherd mix made it to its feet. Jessie ran back to it, taking it back to the ground. In like manner, she again did the same to the second and third dogs, until the three made a break for it, back to their people.

Jessie just stood there, watching the three run off.

"Come on Jessie," my brother said, with a tone of relief and disbelief. Jessie obediently came, allowed us to slip her collar back on, and followed us back down the trail toward home. The three men with their dogs left in the opposite direction.

Jessie was never again forced to prove her loyalty to our family. There was never any doubt in our minds she could do it again.

I'm Not Here

Author Unknown

Don't stand by my grave and weep

For I'm not there, I do not sleep.

I am a thousand winds that blow

I am the diamond glint on the snow

I am the sunlight on the ripened grain

I am the gentle autumn's rain.

When you awaken in morning's hush

I am the swift uplifting rush

Of quiet birds in circle flight

I am the soft stars that shine at night.

Do not stand at my grave and cry

I am not there, I did not die.

Judy

Judy, "My Beautiful Girl"

by Debbie Pedersen

I met Judy back in 1982, when I was asked by a neighbor if I would like to take care of her. Judy was a mare, half Morgan and half Quarter Horse. Her full name was Judy Garland, named after her owner's favorite actress. Our neighbor had seen me riding my friend's pony and came outside to ask if I would like to take care of Judy. Her owner had become ill and was unable to take care of her.

I had always wanted a horse, but was unable to talk my parents into it. So I was very happy to help. Taking care of someone's horse would be the closest thing to having my own. It would be perfect.

Judy and I became close friends. All my spare time was spent with Judy. Then a few months later, her owner had her moved to a stable closer to where I lived. It had a sixty acre pasture and she shared it with twenty other horses.

When my friends and I would go out to catch our horses, most would run around before being caught and then would need a halter and lead rope to be led out to pasture. But not Judy. I only had to call her name and whistle. She would come to me and we'd walk together to the gate. When Judy's ill owner could no longer pay for Judy's board, I got a job to pay for it. When the owner passed away, Judy became mine.

During the summer a friend and I helped out in a nearby rental stable and I'd take Judy with me. We'd get customers mounted on their horses and go out as trail guides. When it was slow, I'd remove Judy's tack and let her graze on the grass around the barn and parking lot. When she finished eating, she would come over to the office and stick her head in the window. If the door had been left open, she'd come right in to hang out with us. People got a big kick out of this.

Many years passed and Judy and I went through a lot together. She was there for me whenever I needed her. Judy and I challenged ourselves many times. I took her to English show jumping events, Western pleasure shows, gymkhana events, and team penning events. We rode in two Fourth of July Parades. My parents said I was probably confusing the poor horse, that she was no longer a young filly. But Judy seemed pleased. She always held her head high and ears forward looking for what was next.

When she was thirty years old, we moved from California to Utah. Instead of riding on the beach, we were going to learn how to ride in the snow. Our first winter I went out to the stables to exercise her while it was snowing. As I walked Judy out the barn door, she looked up at the sky and then backed up into the barn. But I encouraged her and she soon enjoyed it.

We met new friends that were involved in parade and drill events. One day the riding club discovered they were missing a team member and Judy and I were glad to help out. She enjoyed it so much, we joined the club. We participated in one season of showing, then I did not feel comfortable working her so hard anymore. But we still went on trail rides with friends and enjoyed the mountains.

Over the years I owned Judy, I had other horses. But all were sold for one reason or another. While they were younger and some more athletic than Judy, when the time came to decide which one to sell, I could never bring myself to part with her. She meant so much to me.

I decided to adopt a seven-month-old wild Mustang filly named Cricket. Judy really liked her. When they were turned out into the arena together, Judy would watch over her and keep her out of trouble. I moved them to a friend's home with a large corral, where they could be kept together.

The second winter of November 2000, I received a call from my alarmed friend. Judy had not come to the feeder for breakfast and she knew Judy never missed a meal. I rushed over, got out of my car, and called for Judy. When she didn't come, I walked to the corral and found her. Her head hung low and she couldn't walk right. The veterinarian I called said he could be there in two hours. As I stayed with her, waiting for the vet, she got worse and couldn't walk without stumbling or falling down.

When he arrived, I kept telling him that she was fine yesterday, eating, trotting around. The veterinarian said the fact that she was fine the day before and now was going down so fast suggested she had a pituitary gland tumor that had burst. He gave me the option of his taking her to the clinic for tests – or letting her go now. He told me the prognosis was poor.

Judy had been my best friend for twenty years and at the age of forty, she had already lived much longer than most horses. I had to make the hardest decision of my life. I couldn't see putting her through many tests, her struggling for life, just because I didn't want to lose my best friend.

My heart was breaking as I asked the veterinarian to put her down. Once I made that decision, I think Judy felt ready to go. She laid down and seemed to stop fighting for life as he drew up the euthanasia solution. The veterinarian comforted me by explaining that her disease came on so fast, she hadn't suffered until now. For that I was grateful. And while most older horses suffer with arthritis and other lameness problems, Judy never did.

And I'm grateful that Judy got to spend time with Cricket. The spring following Judy's passing was time to break Cricket. I started her out in Judy's hackamore and saddle. After doing a small amount of ground work, I was able to mount Cricket without any problems – not even a buck!

A couple of years have passed and it is still obvious that Judy raised Cricket. She acts like Judy's offspring. While it was very hard losing my best friend after so many years, it still feels like she is with me whenever I am with Cricket.

Nicky

Nicky's Life Was Way Too Short

by Doug Robinson, *Deseret News* columnist

Pardon me if I don't feel like writing today.

I don't feel like trying to be funny, or entertaining, or informative.

I lost an old buddy today. He was my running partner for twelve years. He was my constant companion while I worked in my home office. He followed me around the house so close to my heels that if I suddenly remembered that I had forgotten something and reversed course, I tripped over him.

He didn't have much to say, but he was always good company and always in a good mood. Wherever I was, that's where he wanted to be.

He liked to watch me eat – and vacuumed any crumbs that fell to the floor. He liked to do the dishes after dinner.

He didn't like to wait for me while I wrote my stories – occasionally, I could hear a big sigh – but he bore it with patience. He liked to ride in the car with me and watch the world pass by the window.

Most of all he liked to run. As a high school track coach, I took him to the track for my team's daily workouts. It was his idea of heaven. He liked to race alongside one group of sprinters, and as they crossed the finish he raced to the other side of the track to catch up with another group that was running, and on and on he went.

If I picked up my running shoes in the closet, he paced the floor and whined. We covered a lot of miles together in all kinds of weather. On a couple of occasions, I jogged home carrying him in my arms, his head bobbing up and down. You'd need help, too, if you were running in July while wearing a black fur coat.

I know it's probably not seemly for a grown man to be so attached to a dog, but there it is. Dogs are some of the best people I know, you know what I mean – guileless, happy, eager to please, affectionate. A long time ago, somebody sent me one of those unsolicited e-mails we all get these days, and I thought of it today. It said:

> If you can start the day without caffeine or pep pills; if you can be cheerful, ignoring aches and pains; if you can resist complaining and boring people with your troubles; if you can eat the same food every day and be grateful for it; if you

can understand when loved ones are too busy to give you time; if you can overlook when people take things out on you when, through no fault of yours, something goes wrong; if you can take criticism and blame without resentment; if you can face the world without lies and deceit or drugs and liquor . . . then you are a dog.

We didn't even want him to begin with. He wasn't the prettiest or biggest pup of the litter. He was the runt, a tiny black-and-white Sheltie. But while his siblings were disinterested in their visitors, he vied for our attention. We gave him to our kids on Christmas morning 1990.

He has been with us ever since, except for a few times when we left him behind during an extended vacation. While we were gone, he howled, we were told. When we came home, he raced in circles around us. Our kids grew up with him, dressing him in doll clothes, playing hide and seek and ball games with him (he was useful for retrieving a ball that got away and rolled down the street).

There's just one thing wrong with dogs – They don't live long enough. On Monday afternoon, I took him to the vet. He was very sick with no warning. He could hardly stand. The vet left me alone in the room to say goodbye. I held him in my arms for a long time, talking to him, recalling all the good times we had together.

It was the right thing, the vet assured me. I watched the needle disappear beneath the skin and his eyes slide closed for the last time. We placed him in a box, and I carried him out the back door into a rainy gray day.

Today I'll go for a run. Guess I'll have to go it alone.

Nicky running to heaven

My Best Friend Pepper

by Ashley J. Sprankle

In Loving Memory of "Pepper" aka "Buddy, Bubby"
April 1988 - August 23, 2001

I was young, you were old, we both were the same age.
Every day playing ball, you shake my hand.
Your eyes lit up when you came through our doors
and into loving arms of a family.

You were our pound puppy!
We grew closer to you more each day.
You were a big footed puppy and mama always said
"He's gonna be a big one."

You were my playful pup and best friend.
Black silky coat and big brown eyes,
Always had a silly grin spread across your face.

You even let us dress you up and play weird games with you.
Once you were my cowboy dog in the Kid's Parade.
I could look at your eyes and know that you loved me.

Even when I was having a bad day,
I could come home and snuggle up to you
and that would be okay.

You knew us by name and could find me snuggled in the covers,
to give me a big wet kiss, when daddy would say: "Go find Sissy!"
I will forever love you and forever you'll be my best friend.

Pepper, go and be a hunting dog in heaven and wait for me there where
I can give kisses, hugs and play catch with you once more.
"I was young, you were old, we both were the same age."
I love You!

Puffer & Kamerin

Puffer

by Jane Meyer

Growing up we always had cats. My mom had a beautiful Siamese cat named Ting-a-Ling. She was loving and smart, and she outlasted my older sister's other two cats. I was young when she finally passed away and I begged my parents for a kitten. But they always said no. I kind of adopted strays around the neighborhood, but it just wasn't the same. I begged at least once a day to have my very own kitten, and not just any kitten, it had to be all white.

One night I was sitting at the dinner table doing my homework, and my dad came in from outside all hunched up and clutching his chest, gasping and saying his chest hurt. He flung himself over the table and my homework. I was so scared I didn't realize that a little white puff ball was coming out of his coat. My playful father had been teasing me.

He looked just like a powdered puff except that he had a little black spot on top of his head right between his ears. Hence, this is how I named my beloved white kitten Puffer.

Puffer became my best friend and he was always there for me as I had my bad days and good days growing up in school. He took real good care of me over the years. He would bring me presents of birds, mice, grasshoppers, and spiders. One evening I came home to find him dragging a huge rat downstairs to my room. I don't think he understood why I wouldn't let him put it in my bed.

My family thought I was strange because I would rather talk to Puffer than to them. A very good listener, he was also a talker and a ham. He even could open doors, and if he couldn't he would let you know by meowing until you opened the door.

I loved him very much and he loved me too. He was very loyal to me, as loyal as cats can be. Puffer was a huge tomcat, still all white with a black spot on his head. My busy mom would always think that it was a grease spot, so he got a lot of baths. Each night he would go out, then would return in the early morning to my bed. But one morning he was not there.

A senior in high school and about to graduate, it was a big morning for me. Our school was having a program that night and I was planning to surprise my father with a special song I had been working on for six months. I was leaving for school early to get ready for the big night. Puffer was not there and I kept yelling for him, but he wouldn't come. Finally I looked out at the front yard and then I saw him – lying in the middle of the road on a manhole cover.

Screaming, I raced to him hoping against hope, but knowing he was badly injured. I picked him up very carefully and gently carried him back to the house. About to leave for work, Dad had heard my screams. He took one look at Puffer and said "Get the gun." I was stunned, my heart devastated as my best friend lay badly hurt in my arms. How could my father say such a thing, the very person I had planned to sing the special song for that night?

Mom came to the rescue. She took Puffer from my arms, and quietly said, "Go on to school and I will make sure Puffer is okay." So I left for school, crying my eyes out. Finally, my name was called over the intercom to come to the office. I was terrified they had bad news. But they reassured me that everything was okay with my cat and that I was to call my mother as soon as possible. I made the call.

Mom explained she had taken Puffer to the veterinary hospital and the doctor said he would do everything possible to help him. He said that while he was badly injured, he hoped he could save him. Puffer had lost one eye and suffered a broken jaw and nose; it was like he was split down the middle. He stayed with the doctor for two weeks before I was able to take him home.

His mouth was wired shut so I spent all summer feeding him baby food, and I cleaned his wounds every time he ate. I hoped he wasn't suffering. The doctor said he was surprised that he had lasted this long, that Puffer must really love me, because he wasn't biting me and he let me do all the things I had to do to make him better.

I set up a room just for him so he was being watched all the time. I even slept with him. It was a long recovery, and he eventually grew back all his white hair. Because he had lost a lot of his teeth, I would still hand feed him. I knew it was a long battle for him, and he had the scars to prove it. But he seemed to be coming along just fine.

My sister came back home from Texas and brought her cat Tari with her. Tari and Puffer played well together, but Tari took playful advantage of Puffer's disabilities. Because Puffer was deaf and blind on one side, she would walk very quietly up to that side of Puffer and sit next to him. When he would turn finally and see her there, he would jump sky high. It was fun to watch them play together.

As time passed, the permanent effects of the accident began to settle over me. My precious Puffer got thinner and was sneezing all the time. I finally realized that he was dying. As I watched him suffer, I finally knew that I needed to let him go. But I agonized over the thought of taking my best friend to the veterinarian's office. My mom once again came to the rescue. I could see it was hard for her too. She had taken care of him when I wasn't able to.

Puffer was my best friend, a big part of my life. I'll never, ever forget him.

Sophie

Our Beautiful Sophie

by Marisa McKinnon and Michele McKinnon

My sister Michele gave me this poem the day after Sophie died. I was in such deep despair at the loss of my sweet baby and faithful companion that I was hysterical. My family didn't know what to do to help me.

I thought that nobody could possibly understand how much pain I was in. Michele wanted to do something to show me that she understood and felt my pain as well. And as a result, she wrote this poem. When I came home and saw it framed with a picture of Sophie on the kitchen table, I broke down. It seemed that she knew exactly what I needed. She found a way to get through to me when I was emotionally unreachable.

She showed me that I was not alone in loving and missing Sophie. Sophie impacted the lives of all who knew her.

Our beautiful Sophie so sweet and so kind,
Although she is gone, she holds in our minds.

Marisa and Sophie, oh what a pair!
We will always remember the memories they share.

So vibrant, so young, and full of life...
How can I help you to get through the strife?

Her death was so sudden, so unexpected.
This horrible tragedy cannot be corrected.

I want to reverse it, but what can I do?
I know your heart is broken, I give mine to you.

Although we may travel both near and far,
We will always remember her wherever we are.

And though our sweet Sophie was taken away,
I know we will see her again someday.

What a wonderful companion with so many charms.
What a wonderful day when you next hold her in your arms!

Our Sophie was taken away with much haste
Such an outstanding dog that can never be replaced

She was a sweet little spirit, she gave us endless love.
She now lives as a queen up in heaven above.

Section 2

Goodbye Good Friend

Pug

A Letter to Pug

by Alan Cunningham

My dearest Pug,

Quietly you left me a year ago. I still miss you deeply and wonder if the tears will ever go away. Probably not. I trust you are happy, running and playing in the meadows with Dad by your side. I imagine that he enjoys your companionship and still rubs your belly. I recall how you would position yourself in front of him, roll over on your back, and beg for belly rubs. And you always got them too, didn't you.

Oh, how I vividly recollect so many beautiful memories about you, my precious angel. The day is still fresh in my mind when I brought you home from the pet store curled up daintily on my lap. You caught my eye the instant I saw you. Your exquisite, black, almond-shaped eyes beckoned with curiosity and innocent mischievousness.

I carried you home and gave you to Dad. Even though he was in a wheelchair his eyes danced with joy as he held you in his lap. Those large, Boston Terrier eyes gazing at a new and exciting world.

And although I gave you to Dad, you were mine. You tugged on my heartstrings from the beginning. The first night that you slept by my side, I felt like I was sleeping with an angel. I soon learned that "you do not own a dog, the dog owns you."

You remained by my side, my angel, almost constantly. Do you remember the interview I had with the veterinary state licensing committee? What an unprofessional experience! I angrily marched out from meeting with them and then suddenly wondered if my chances of obtaining a license to practice veterinary medicine would ever be realized. As I hopelessly began to sob you were there to lick away the tears. Somehow you comforted me when no one else could.

And the time we hiked into Rainbow Bridge National Monument. How careless of me to attempt such a challenge by myself. But you were there with me. When it became cold and dark, and I got lost, you led us out of the merciless, desolate canyons. Step by tiny step you would proceed, and then frequently stop and glance back at me to see that I was okay, and then venture on. Eventually we made it out of the chaos of massive, dark canyons. You were my little wonder.

Someday, in the not too distant future, I hope that we can again cross Rainbow Bridge together. I will always remember the morning I took you to see Dad in his casket at the mortuary. I wanted you to know he wasn't coming back. I held you in my arms and you just silently and motionlessly stared at him. Then we quietly left. If you could only tell me what you really saw on that day. A whisper into the future perhaps?

Unlike the other dogs, you always maintained your own agenda. When we would go jogging you would quickly become disinterested and venture on your own explorations. Unfortunately, because of your enormous curiosity, you got swept down the Jordan River.

When the other dogs and I returned from jogging, you were no where to be found. We frantically searched for you, but with no success. I agonized that I had lost you forever.

Thank goodness the fisherman saw you and pulled you from the cold, muddy water. You were exhausted when he returned you to us.

Mom said that you knew I wouldn't give up on finding you, and that you loved me so much in return that you refused to give up as well. On that eventful day you taught me that unconditional love grows even stronger when it is reciprocated.

I remember the sad day you ran in front of the car, while fearlessly chasing the unwelcome dog out of the yard. You could not use your right back leg and you painfully looked at me with questioning eyes.

Then, a year afterward you were diagnosed with a blood clot in your right front leg. Again, you stared at me with wondering eyes. Those beautiful, almond-shaped, enormous eyes that attracted me to you were now filled with pain.

With all my energy and veterinary expertise, I could not save you or remove you from the pain. I am so sorry. You quietly left me early on Sunday morning of August 11, 2002. Softly you gasped a few tiny breaths as I gently held you in my arms and then you peacefully closed your eyes.

My seemingly empty world was shattered. I wanted to accompany you. You had always been by my side. I could not easily release you from my life. But, it was not my time to pass over the Rainbow Bridge with you.

In your own loving way, you had prepared a legion of angels to watch over me – namely C.C., Brownie, Golden, Aspen, and Moose. They are all doing fine. Aspen, however, being three-legged and older, is having a difficult time walking. I suspect you are preparing a place for her soon.

And how I cherish the two little angels you have sent to me – Angel and Chloe. Angel seems so much like you with her independent spirit. While Chloe, being a Boston Terrier, has the same grunts and snorts that you so loudly displayed. How refreshing it is to occasionally view the world through the carefree eyes of a puppy!

You would be so proud of C.C.. She has stepped into your role of matriarch with determined responsibility and grace. When you died, her face turned prematurely gray almost overnight. We all miss you. Mom visits your grave daily. She says, "I had a long talk with Pug this morning and she is doing fine." You will forever remain in our hearts.

In a few weeks, I will run the New York City Marathon. And even though you thought aimless running was silly, I hope that you will be by my side the entire 26.2 miles. When I am tired and discouraged, I will look down and see you smiling cheerfully up into my face. And I will not be alone because I will have a precious angel by my side.

I dearly miss you, Pug. You are my sweetest angel and forever love. You will never be absent from my heart.

"And know you're there, a breath away's not far to where you are."

Legion of Angels

Be Mine

by Alan Cunningham

Child

Please don't go away
Oh why can't you stay
And be mine
be mine

Why did you have to go
You know I loved you so
For all time
all time

And as the world will see
Our love will always be
So divine
so divine
Be mine

Adult

All creatures great and small
Our god had made them all
For mankind
mankind

The waters of the sea
The land and skies will be
Their home
their home

So we must share our love
With our friends from above
So true
so true
Be mine

Youth

Please don't go away
Our love will ever stay
Always
always

You are my truest friend
We'll see it to the end
We will
we will

Until on angels wings
Our god to heaven brings
You home
you home
Be mine

Lost Companion

So please don't cry for me
Our love will always be
Yours and mine
and mine

You knew I had to go
And that I loved you so
For all time
all time

And as the world will see
Our love will always be
So divine
divine
Be mine, Be, be, be....mine

Friends in Heaven

Yoshi

Yoshi

by Alan Cunningham

Yoshi delicately placed soft prints on my heart last April. When I arrived for night shift at the emergency clinic, I was given her story. Yoshi was a beautiful, nine year old spayed Boxer. She had been transported to the emergency clinic from her regular veterinary clinic for seizure observation.

Unfortunately, she did not respond favorably to the seizure medications – valium, phenobarbital. The only way to keep her relaxed was with heavy doses of anesthetic drugs. As the drugs wore off, the seizure activity would resume.

Being older for a Boxer, and non-responsive to the seizure medications, the owners were given a guarded to poor prognosis for Yoshi.

"Often times we become concerned about brain tumors when animals don't respond to regular medication," the previous veterinarian had cautioned.

As a result, the owners had decided to wait and see how Yoshi would respond one more time after she awoke from the heavy sedation.

"If she continues to exhibit seizure activity, the owners would like to have her euthanized," I was informed.

Cautiously, I observed Yoshi as the anesthetic began to wear off. Slowly, with gradually increasing disoriented movement, she began to paddle with her front legs. Sadly, the seizure activity had continued.

I phoned her owners. "Hi, this is Dr. Cunningham. Yoshi is beginning to awaken and is showing seizure activity. What would you like me to do?"

After a long moment and what sounded like choked-back tears, she said, "We would like to end her suffering and have her euthanized."

"I appreciate your grief and will honor your request," I sadly replied. Suddenly, I felt burdened and heavy-hearted. I would be the last threshold between life and death for Yoshi.

Slowly, I knelt down and opened the door to her cage and called her name. "Yoshi." I sat on the floor waiting for her response.

Awkwardly, she crawled from the ground level steel cage and purposefully crept toward me. Then she did something I will always remember. She slowly climbed into my lap and leaned her head against my stomach.

She knew...All she wanted was to be held one last time.

As I cradled her in my lap, I realized that we silently shared the gift of peace with each other for a brief moment.

For as long as I practice veterinary medicine, I will always be amazed by the understanding that animals have of euthanasia. They seem to know. For a short time they transcend the debilitating and painful illness and possess a look of resolve, dignified silence, a purposeful glimpse beyond earthly boundaries, and simply and quietly give up the mortal fight.

Many times they are thought of as the silent third party. Too often they sink from the equation when theirs is the ultimate price to pay. And for the seeming blasphemous and sometimes detached arrogance of man, the animals understand the sacrifice that they must offer...must give.

Carefully, I lifted Yoshi's limp body from my lap and then softly whispered into her ear, "Please say hi to Pug for me."

Wings to Fly

by Isabel M. Gordon

For all the joy you've given me

For the glory days gone by

My best and final gift my love,

I grant you wings to fly.

Used with permission. Isabel M. Gordon, Phoenix Rising Publications, 1994.

Dove in Flight

Preparing Children for Pet Loss

by Marty Tousley

Be open and honest. If the pet is terminally ill, death is pending and euthanasia is necessary, tell your children as soon as possible so they will hear it first from you and not from someone else. If they ever discover that you distorted the truth or lied to them, they'll have a great deal of trouble trusting you again.

Offer basic, age-appropriate explanations, and be available for questions. Children need to know that grief is normal and necessary, and it's all right to feel sad. Make certain they know that it is the pet's death (not something your children did or failed to do) that makes you sad. Explain what "dead" means (the animal's body stops working and won't work anymore), and make it clear that death is not the same as sleeping (when we sleep our body is still working, just resting). Avoid the common phrase for euthanasia, "put to sleep" as it can trigger sleep problems or intense anxiety over surgery and anesthesia. Better to say the pet will be helped to die peacefully and without pain. Don't say that the pet has "passed away," "left us" or "gone on." Such phrases imply the pet is on a trip and will return, leave children feeling rejected or abandoned, or encourage them to go searching for the lost pet or hold out hope for its return.

Help young children understand why euthanasia is necessary. Explain that their pet may be suffering from old age (when an animal gets very, very, very old, its body wears out and stops working); terminal illness (because the disease couldn't be stopped, the pet is very, very sick; its body has worn out and has stopped working);an accident (a terrible thing happened, the pet's body was badly hurt and couldn't be fixed; it stopped working).

Avoid telling children that their pet was so good or so special that God wants it to be with Him in heaven. Children may become angry with God or fear that they (or you) will be chosen next.

Don't blame the veterinarian. As a result your children may develop fear of veterinarians and other health care givers.

Include children in the euthanasia decision. Never euthanize a family pet without telling your children first, even if they're away from home. Children need help in understanding why the decision has to be made and a feeling that they've participated in making it. They also need an opportunity to say good-bye and make the most of whatever time they may have left with the pet.

Prepare children ahead of time as to what to expect. Hold a family meeting and discuss the veterinarian's diagnosis, the pet's prognosis and the cost of treatments and care, including side effects and the pet's quality of life. Schedule a visit to the veterinarian's office to learn about the euthanasia procedure itself and answer any questions you or your children may have. (Find out in advance how it will be done and where; how long it takes; if the pet will feel any pain; whether the family can be present; what will be done with the pet's remains afterward.)

Encourage children's involvement in the pet's euthanasia. Let them be present during the procedure if they so choose. The reality of a peaceful death is far less traumatic to children than their terrible fantasy of it. Encourage children to see their pet after death, which reinforces the reality and removes the mystery and fear of death.

Explain what will happen to the pet's remains. If you plan to have your pet cremated, explain that your pet will be taken to a pet crematory, a place where the pet's body will be turned into ashes. Then your family will take those ashes and (scatter them; bury them in the backyard; keep them in an urn; etc.).

Plan a memorial ritual. Decide in advance what you will do with your pet's remains, how you'll honor your pet's life and keep its memory alive. Encourage activities to help your children experience and express their love and grief (drawing or painting pictures; compiling an album, scrapbook or memory box; viewing videos or home movies; writing or sharing memories; planting a shrub or tree; reading books on pet loss).

Respect and encourage your children's needs to express and share feelings of sadness. When you bring up the subject, you're showing your own willingness to talk about it. When in doubt about your children's thoughts and feelings, ask. Don't feel as if you must have all the answers; sometimes just listening is enough. Expect that young children will ask and need answers to the same questions over and over again. Don't cut off their feelings by noting how well your children are handling their grief or how brave or strong they are. Let them see you upset and crying, which implies that it's all right to cry for those we love and lose.

Respect the feelings of other family members. Recognize that not everyone in the family is equally attached to the pet and that not everyone shows their feelings or grieves in the same way. Note: Marty Tousley is a hospice bereavement counselor who specializes in pet loss and writes about various aspects of grief. To get in touch with Marty or obtain more information about her works, visit www.griefhealing.com. tousley@aol.com.

(Based on *Children and Pet Loss: A Guide for Helping*, by Marty Tousley, and used with permission)

Dr. Moss & Sam

The Price of a Dog

by Neil Moss DVM

"Doc, If it were your dog, what would you do?"
"If this broken leg we found on the road just now were yours;
If this cancerous lump, invading; or these twisted bowels were yours,
what would you do?"
Why does that question always and so painfully drop upon my vulnerability?
My table's dented enough with my fees,
and has only just been cleaned.
And why do they ask from that sea of children's eyes
which plead for me to be divine?
Compassion holds me ransomed once again.
And so, from my bedside, feeling, I dispense;
then unobtrusively lay the dog aside.
They're supposed to make this choice,
but there's a price on those bowels;
and I'm not supposed to mend that bone for free,
despite the tugging eyes.
So I fish with gentle words, and offer balm;
and tell them it's OK to take his life;
"He won't feel a thing,"
as he sinks from the equation.
This universal pain of loss is theirs, not mine;
but those tissued silences, and the cremated sobs,
and once again I'll wear the coat that grows
like the mass that took his life.
And so I ask –
Is mine an act of godliness?
Or one of blasphemy?

St. Peter

Author Unknown

I explained to St. Peter,

I'd rather stay here,

Outside the pearly gate.

I won't be a nuisance,

I won't even bark,

I'll be very patient and wait.

I'll be here, chewing on a celestial bone,

No matter how long you may be.

I'd miss you so much, if I went in alone,

It wouldn't be heaven for me.

Pug with Guardian Angel

Overcoming the Grief of Beloved Animal Companions That Have Passed Away

by Alan Cunningham

Grieving is a natural part of beloved animal companion loss. Dr. Elisabeth Kubler-Ross published a famous book entitled "On Death and Dying." She outlined five stages of bereavement. These stages include denial, anger, bargaining, depression, and acceptance.

Presently, grief counselors have modified Dr. Kubler-Ross' five stages. They present the grieving process as four tasks. They include:

1. Accept the reality of loss. Intense waves of emotion (hearing or seeing the departed animal) will eventually pass.

2. Experience the painful feeling associated with the loss-grief and sadness are allowable.

3. Adjust to an environment in which the deceased is missing-ultimately we have to put away the food dish, the leash, and the toys and in time (not necessarily today or even weeks), we will adjust.

4. Reinvest in life—when the time is right, be willing to love again. Obtain another pet, knowing that in reality you will most likely see it die also. Accept what's lovable in the new animal. Remember not to use it as a replacement for the previous animal but instead as a way of honoring its memory.

A few practical ways to cope with animal companion loss are listed:

1. Give yourself permission to grieve.

2. Take time to heal.

3. Know that guilt often accompanies grief.

4. Find a special way to say goodbye. Write a letter to your animal companion, or display a photo or drawing.

5. Memorialize your animal companion. Assemble a scrapbook, plant a tree or flower, write, or donate money in his or her name to a charity for animals or animal loss support hot lines.

6. Find other people to talk with candidly about your grief.

7. Be good to yourself. Grief drains energy. Get adequate rest, eat healthy, exercise, meditate.

8. Do at least one thing each day that brings you joy.

9. Allow yourself to laugh.

10. Submit an obituary in tribute of your animal. Several newspapers offer "Pet Remembrances." If your newspaper doesn't provide this service, encourage them to do so.

Grief is very personal, and we must experience at least some of these steps before we can proceed with our lives after the loss of a beloved animal companion. Crying or anger, for example, is not always necessary for everyone. An individual's own way of grieving is acceptable.

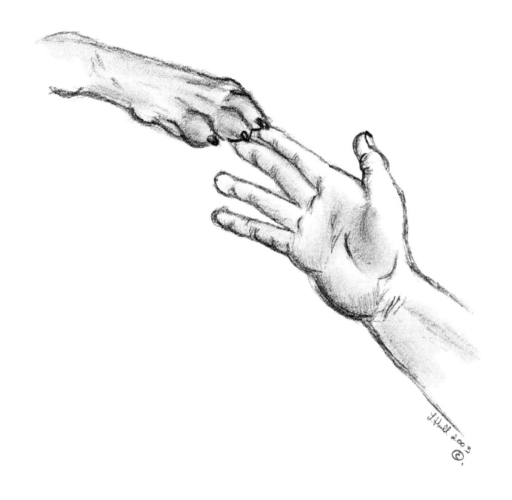

Letting Go

Additional Information on Pet Loss and Grief Support

by Alan Cunningham

The loss of an animal companion can be profound and significant. To many people, the loss of a beloved animal friend is similar to the loss of a family member. The resulting grief should be recognized as normal and necessary.

Unfortunately, this unique grief – often identified as disenfranchised grief because others don't understand and appreciate it – is met with such phrases as "get over it – it's just an animal," or "why don't you replace it with another animal?" Many people do not understand or appreciate the very real grief associated with the loss of an animal companion. And neither do they realize that the unique relationship of the animal cannot be replaced with another pet.

As a result, many people feel alone and isolated by society in the grief associated with the loss of a precious animal companion. Society must realize that grief, involved with the loss of an animal companion, is perfectly normal and valid. Also, it is important to recognize that several support groups are available to help and to actively listen with an empathetic attitude.

Grief is normal and unique – we can't change or interfere with that fact. People tend to handle the various stages of grief, such as denial, anger, bargaining, depression, guilt, and ultimately acceptance, in different and personalized styles. But just as important as it is to experience the various stages of grief, it is also important to not get caught up in them so much that we forget the process of grief itself. For example, people can become so involved and locked into guilt that they overlook the real and ongoing process of grief. In time, we must let go of each individual stage of grief and progress to the ultimate goal of healthy acceptance.

Often times linking or transitional objects help to provide closure with the loss of an animal companion. These linking objects may include a lock of hair, a paw print, identification tags, or photographs. Ceremonialization of the animal friend, through transitional items, is especially helpful to children that may have difficulty understanding the permanence of death.

As far as children – particularly those less than five to seven years of age – death of a pet must be approached frankly, honestly, and in terms that they can understand. For example, when an animal dies, tell them it isn't breathing, or moving, and is dead. Misleading analogies or phrases such as "it is asleep, or gone" can be troubling and confusing to them. They often attend such phrases with fear to go to sleep, or they may wonder where the animal has gone to and want to search for it.

People who are more at risk for difficulty with the loss of an animal companion are often single, without extended family or friends, and view the animal as their only real friend or companion. They often identify the animal as their soul mate or lifesaver. Or, perhaps they identify it with another loved one that has died. For instance a dog belonged to a husband – the husband died – and now the wife associates the loss of the dog with the death of her husband – only compounding the grief.

Finally, in extreme circumstances, some pet owners may become suicidal with the death of an animal companion. Critical suicidal risks can be ascertained by asking two questions: 1. on a scale of 1–10 what are your tendencies to want to commit suicide, and 2. on a scale of 1–10 what degree do you plan on acting upon these feelings. People with a higher level of wanting to act upon their feelings are at higher risk of committing suicide and should be taken more seriously and provided with immediate professional help.

In conclusion, grief over the death of a beloved animal companion is normal and healthy. Sharing these feelings, with someone who is willing to actively listen with an empathetic attitude, is helpful in validating these feelings and working through to a healthy acceptance and resolution. Many support organizations are available to help. Please take advantage of their assistance. Local veterinary clinics can provide contact information.

Reference Source: Lagoni, Butler. Hetts. "The Human-Animal Bond and Grief."1994. W.B. Saunders Company.

Grief Counseling

by Alan Cunningham

Listen, Listen, and Listen.

As pet loss grief counselors, we need to remember three lessons: listen, listen, and listen. Let me explain:

1. Most people are capable of making rationale, healthy decisions on their own – they just want someone to actively and empathetically listen to them. This process helps to validate their feelings. When a person is grieving, we are there to listen. If they are silent, we respect that silence and remain quiet until they give us permission to comment. At that point we briefly summarize back to them what they have just told us. This helps them to understand that we have actively listened to them and that we are genuinely concerned. And sometimes this is all the individual needs for healthy resolution.

2. Grief is very personal and unique. We do not have the right to take away from someone's grief by saying "I know how you feel." Because we don't. Instead we listen, and, if asked, we offer "It must be difficult for you," or "I know of other people that have experienced similar events." or "I appreciate your grief."

3. As counselors, we are not trained in behavioral modification or therapy. Again, our main responsibility is to listen. We may offer suggestions or guidelines, if asked, but we are not to provide answers. Other professionals are available for people that need more advanced counseling.

Grief counseling, especially in children under five years of age, may be different. They do not understand the permanence of death. And to many, it is their first exposure to death. They need to understand that their beloved pet will not be returning. They need to be given options to help them with the closure, such as memorializing the lost pet through pictures, obituaries, planting a tree or flower in the pet's name, or having a funeral for the lost animal. Many other options are also available to help with closure.

For those pet owners that are contemplating euthanasia of an animal or who have euthanized an animal, they need to realize three goals in order for the experience to feel right to them:

1. Clients must believe that the choice is theirs.

2. They must believe that the choice is the right one.

3. They must be adequately informed about the procedure and what to expect.

In summary, our main goal as pet loss grief counselors is to listen, listen, and listen. Remember, young children view pet loss differently. Owners must feel in control and educated about euthanasia of a pet in order for the experience to be right for them.

Euthanasia

by Alan Cunningham

Stedman's Twenty Second Edition Medical Dictionary defines euthanasia as a quiet, painless death. Euthanasia is the intentional putting to death, by artificial means, of persons or animals with incurable or painful disease.

Owners, who are considering euthanasia for their companion animals, must realize three needs for the experience to feel right. Initially, they must believe that the choice is theirs. Secondly, they must sense that the choice is the right one. And finally, they must be informed about the procedure and what to expect.

First, how do animal owners recognize when it is time for euthanasia? Most veterinarians will say if an animal is constantly painful, even when treated with pain medications, unhappy and unable to move, or eat, and to interact pleasantly with others, then it is time.

Pet owners are encouraged to be with their pet when it is euthanized. The final act of companionship tends to provide a closing bond of comfort. Pet owners may hold or touch their animal friend during the procedure.

When the animal is severely painful or anxious, the veterinarian will administer a sedative or tranquilizer to help calm it before the euthanasia is performed.

Some owners prefer to have their pet euthanized at home in familiar and comfortable surroundings with family members present. Or occasionally the animal will be too big and incapacitated to move to the veterinary clinic. In this case, some veterinarians may accommodate or suggest a traveling veterinarian that can provide these services.

The drug used for euthanasia is sodium pentobarbital (beuthanasia). When administered intravenously, at high concentrations, pentobarbital causes instantaneous, painless death by severely depressing the respiratory center. Death may be slower or the injection painful if the substance is given perivascularly or outside the vein. Therefore, an intravenous catheter is sometimes placed to assure a painless and effective administration.

Sometimes an animal may be so sick and dehydrated that it is difficult to locate an adequate vein to administer the euthanasia solution. Then the drug is given intra cardiac or intra abdominal. If it is given intra abdominally, into the liver for example, the death will come more slowly, about ten minutes, but the event is still peaceful.

Several options are available after the animal is euthanized. Depending upon the living situations of the owner and the city ordinances, the animal may be taken home and buried or interned in a pet cemetery.

Other options include leaving the body at the veterinary clinic. The clinic has arrangements for weekly retrieval by a crematorium. The body is then cremated privately if the owner requests return of the ashes, or it is cremated with a group of others.

When a private cremation is requested, the ashes are placed in a personalized urn or container. Many services also return a paw print of the pet. Some people may keep a lock of hair or the animal's collar.

During and after the euthanasia it is okay for the owner to cry. Grief is perfectly normal and essential. Sometimes the veterinarian also becomes emotionally involved; it's hard not to. The owners should feel comfortable to spend time afterward to say goodbye to their beloved pet.

As a veterinarian, I recognize the difficulty of euthanizing a pet companion. The procedure is often accompanied with grief, guilt, and a feeling that we are letting a loved one down. But when a beloved pet is incurable, and chronically painful, the blessed relief from suffering is welcome. And in a sense we grant our animal angel "wings to fly."

The veterinary clinic should be able to provide pet loss support counseling and hot lines to help with pet loss and the healing process. Essentially the owners need to know that someone is available to actively listen to their grief following the loss of a beloved animal companion.

Rose and Baby's Breath

Belker

by Author Unknown

Being a veterinarian, I had been called to examine a ten year old Irish Wolfhound named Belker. The dog's owners, Ron, his wife, Lisa, and their little boy, Shane were all very attached to Belker and were hoping for a miracle. I examined Belker and found he was dying of cancer. I told the family there were no miracles left for Belker, and offered to perform the euthanasia procedure for the old dog in their home.

As we made arrangements, Ron and Lisa told me they thought it would be good for their four year old son to observe the procedure. They felt Shane could learn something from the experience.

The next day I felt the familiar catch in my throat as Belker's family surrounded him. Shane seemed so calm, petting the old dog for the last time. I wondered if he understood what was going on.

Within a few minutes, Belker slipped peacefully away. The little boy seemed to accept Belker's transition without any difficulty or confusion.

We sat together for a while after Belker's death, wondering aloud about the sad fact that animal lives are shorter than human lives.

Shane, who had been listening quietly, piped up, "I know why."

Startled, we all turned to him.

What came out of his mouth next stunned me. I'd never heard a more comforting explanation.

He said, "Everybody is born so that they can learn how to live a good life, like loving everybody and being nice, right?"

The four year old continued, "Well, animals already know how to do that, so they don't have to stay here as long as people do."

Just A Minute

by Diane Hunter

Just a minute, don't you all know?
This is my mother and I loved her so.

Just a minute, God will wait.
Soon the others can celebrate.

But for now, just a minute, can't you see?
Letting her go is agony!

OK, I cry! Here she comes.
Ring the bells, sound the drums.

Take her hand, hold her tight.
Walk slowly, follow the light.

Now let her dance, she feels no more pain.
Until reverence must prevail again.

Then quietly listen, his footsteps sound near.
Be still till he comes – Ah he is here!

Just a minute, he says loud and clear.
It is now time for me and my child to be near.

Just a minute.

Note: While Diane wrote this poem and song in tribute to her mother, Afton Southall Saylor, she feels that it can be used universally with the passing of any loved one.

Section 3

The Journey

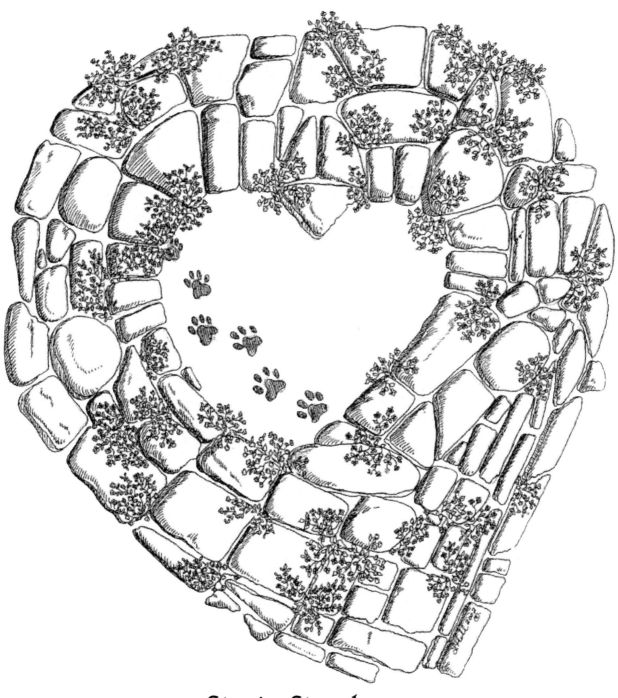

Stepping Stone Journey

Stepping Stone Journey is symbolic of the journey through life's trials—one step at a time—
and the unconditional involvement, loyalty, and protection of beloved animal companions.

The Journey

by Crystal Ward Kent

When you bring a pet into your life, you begin a journey.
A journey that will bring you more love and devotion than you have ever known,
yet will also test your strength and courage. If you allow, the journey will teach you many things,
about life, about yourself, and most of all, about love. You will come away changed forever,
for one soul cannot touch another without leaving its mark.

Along the way, you will learn much about savoring life's simple pleasures – jumping in leaves,
snoozing in the sun, the joys of puddles, and even the satisfaction of a good scratch behind the ears.
If you spend much time outside, you will be taught how to truly experience every element,
for no rock, leaf, or log will go unexamined, no rustling bush will be overlooked,
and even the very air will be inhaled, pondered, and noted as being full of valuable information.

Your pace may be slower, except when heading home to the food dish,
but you will become a better naturalist, having been taught by an expert in the field.
Too many times we hike on automatic pilot, our goal being to complete the trail rather than
enjoy the journey. We miss the details: the colorful mushrooms on the rotting log,
the honeycomb in the old maple snag, the hawk feather caught on a twig.

Once we walk as a dog does, we discover a whole new world.
We stop; we browse the landscape, we kick over leaves, peek in tree holes, look up, down, all around.
And we learn what any dog knows that nature has created a marvelously complex world
that is full of surprises, that each cycle of the seasons bring ever changing wonders,
each day an essence all its own.

Even from indoors you will find yourself more attuned to the world around you.
You will find yourself watching: summer insects collecting on a screen; how bizarre they are; how
many kinds there are or noting the flick and flash of fireflies through the dark. You will stop to
observe the swirling dance of windblown leaves, or sniff the air after a rain. It does not matter that
there is no objective in this; the point is in the doing, in not letting life's most important details slip by.

You will find yourself doing silly things that your pet-less friends might not understand: spending thirty minutes in the grocery aisle looking for the cat food brand your feline must have, buying dog birthday treats, or driving around the block an extra time because your pet enjoys the ride. You will roll in the snow, wrestle with chewie toys, bounce little rubber balls till your eyes cross, and even run around the house trailing your bathrobe tie with a cat in hot pursuit, all in the name of love.

Your house will become muddier and hairier. You will wear less dark clothing and buy more lint rollers. You may find dog biscuits in your pocket or purse, and feel the need to explain that an old plastic shopping bag adorns your living room rug because your cat loves the crinkly sound. You will learn the true measure of love. The steadfast, undying kind that says, "It doesn't matter where we are or what we do, or how life treats us as long as we are together."

Respect this always. It is the most precious gift any living soul can give another. You will not find it often among the human race. And you will learn humility. The look in my dog's eyes often made me feel ashamed. Such joy and love at my presence. She saw not some flawed human who could be cross and stubborn, moody or rude, but only her wonderful companion. Or maybe she saw those things and dismissed them as mere human foibles, not worth considering, and so chose to love me anyway.

If you pay attention and learn well, when the journey is done, you will be not just a better person, but the person your pet always knew you to be. The one they were proud to call beloved friend. I must caution you that this journey is not without pain. Like all paths of true love, the pain is part of loving. For as surely as the sun sets, one day your dear animal companion will follow a trail you cannot yet go down. And you will have to find the strength and love to let them go.

A pet's time on earth is far too short, especially for those that love them. We borrow them, really, just for a while, and during these brief years they are generous enough to give us all their love, every inch of their spirit and heart, until one day there is nothing left. The cat that only yesterday was a kitten is all too soon old and frail and sleeping in the sun. The young pup of boundless energy now wakes up stiff and lame, the muzzle gone to gray.

Deep down we somehow always knew that this journey would end. We knew that if we gave our hearts they would be broken. But give them we must for it is all they ask in return. When the time comes, and the road curves ahead to a place we cannot see, we give one final gift and let them run on ahead, young and whole once more. "God speed, good friend," we say, until our journey comes full circle and our paths cross again.

Simple Things: A Lullaby

by Alan Cunningham

Why did you have to go?
You know I love you so...go on, go on, go on.
When will we meet again?
When can I hold you next to me, to me, to me.

The journey goes full circle
til we both will meet again.
Beneath the stone called Rainbow Bridge
to reach the wondrous end.

When did I hold you last?
Or did time slip away...hold on, hold on, hold on.
These are the simple things,
That make life beautiful day, by day, by day.

The soul would have no rainbow
had the eye no tear to cry.
My best and final gift my love
I grant you wings to fly.

These are the simple things,
That make life beautiful day, by day, by day.

Rainbow Bridge

Small Wonders

by Alan Cunningham

Rainbow Bridge (Nonnezoshe), nestled in the protective shadows of Navajo Mountain near the Utah and Arizona border, is the world's largest natural stone bridge. The sandstone arch is two hundred and ninety feet tall with a two hundred and seventy-five foot long span. This is large enough to comfortably fit the entire United States Capitol Building underneath.

The Navajo Indians consider the multi-hued sandstone arch to be sacred. Legend holds that Nonnezoshe (rainbow turned to stone) was created when an inchworm caterpillar (shooting worm) stretched itself across the canyon. The resulting span provided a bridge to the Navajo Twin Gods.

Many traditional American Indians have superstitious beliefs about the natural archway. To some, it is the sign of the sun's course over the earth. Others consider the Rainbow Bridge to be the doorway between life and death. Still others believe that it is forbidden to walk underneath the sacred arch without saying a special prayer.

Since the land between Navajo Mountain and Rainbow Bridge is also considered sacred, the national park service has officially eliminated all maps and pamphlets that explain how to hike to the monument. Presently the rugged trails into the stone arch are still open to the public, but are extremely difficult to maneuver.

"One can easily get lost in the vast canyons leading to Rainbow Bridge," wrote Zane Grey. The great western novelist described his journey in 1913 as one of the worst trails in the West. He recorded the land to be a "chaos of a million canyons, where a man became nothing."

In late September 1995, my friend, Rob, and I challenged ourselves to hike the sixteen miles into the desolate canyons of Navajo Nation. Being somewhat adventurous, stubborn, and foolhardy (simply put — men,) we chose to traverse the poorly marked, rugged trails leading into the sacred structure, rather than to procure a simpler tourist boat ride on Lake Powell into the natural wonder.

We enthusiastically started our journey early in the morning. The expansive blue sky was crisp and clear. Armed with hiking gear, we looked forward to experiencing the pristine scenery.

The massive, sheer canyon cliffs were vibrant with brilliant sandstone orange, red, yellow, black, and vermilion. The barren landscape of red sand was accented with sagebrush, cedars, volcanic rock, and a few cottonwood trees near the occasional streams. Some of the leaves had already turned a stunning amber.

Of course, my constant companion, Pug, accompanied us. Initially she was aglow with puppy enthusiasm as she explored the new surroundings, smiling and running up and down the obscure trails. Eventually, however, she tired. Convincingly she situated herself in front of me and pleadingly looked up.

"Okay little girl, I'll carry you," I resigned.

Pug beamed as she was now able to get a better view of the scenery without expending the least bit of energy. Sometimes I would try to cradle her next to my shoulder. But she wouldn't allow it. She must face forward in order to see what waited ahead.

Therefore she rested, her front legs draped across my outstretched left arm, and her hindquarters nestled on my right arm. When I became tired, she would briefly tolerate walking and then would again move in front of me, stop, and beg to be carried. Again, I picked her up and carried her.

Onward we steadfastly marched. The mid-day sun became uncomfortably hot. Eventually we arrived at the top of a narrow, rocky trail tightly clinging to the side of the steep cliffs. Pug and I cautiously continued the weaving descent downwards, but Rob would not move.

"What's wrong," I yelled back.

"I can't do it," Rob replied.

"Do what?" I asked.

"I'm afraid of heights," he admitted.

The mischievous smirk on my face soon disappeared. Returning back to Rob I offered to let him hold onto my arm so that we could descend the perilous canyon path together.

"No, you and Pug go on. I'll meet you back at the campsite where the truck is."

Warily, I agreed. "Pug and I will continue on then." Silently, we watched as the physical giant of a man slowly turned around and left us.

Early afternoon beckoned and we still hadn't reached Rainbow Bridge. "Just a little way further," I encouraged. Pug just looked up at me with complete confidence.

"As long as you carry me, I'm with you all the way buddy," her eyes seemed to convey.

Finally, we discovered a small canyon with running water. We drank and rested. I noted the afternoon shade was stretching across the canyon. "The sun is starting to descend, Pug, I think we better turn around."

Disappointed, we turned back. On another future occasion, Pug and I were able to successfully reach Rainbow Bridge. This time, however, we didn't. After filling our water container in the refreshing stream, we started our lone, arduous journey back.

My goal was to ascend out of the deep canyon my friend had left us at before nightfall. I decided that particular area of the hike would be much too treacherous to navigate in the dark. Fortunately, we climbed out of the canyon as dusk approached. The remaining trail back to camp was fairly flat and more easily passable.

The vast skies gradually continued to darken and storm clouds gathered. Then it began to rain. Unfortunately, I had no flashlight. The poorly marked trails became impossible to follow in the dark.

"Pug, I need your help to find our way back. I'm lost and can't see very well. You're going to have to walk ahead and guide us to camp."

Exhausted, I placed her on the ground. She looked up at me as if to say, "We can do it buddy." She shook the rain off herself, and then confidently marched ahead, one step at a time. I followed with complete trust in her. Frequently she would stop, look back at me to see that I was okay, and then proceed forward.

After several hours in the darkened, rainy evening, we arrived to the path that led to our campsite and truck. Not once, during that entire time, did Pug beg me to carry her. And when she safely guided us to the roughened dirt road she began to walk faster. "We made it buddy," she seemed to rejoice, "I'm so excited to be back!"

"Pug, you are my little wonder," I proudly acknowledged to her.

Rob greeted us at the truck. He had prepared dinner. "I was worried if you would make it back in the dark."

I told him about Pug being our guide.

He grinned, "She is some dog."

"Yes," I agreed. Truly she had been my guiding light and faithful companion. I also realized that without Pug, alone in the merciless canyons, I would have become "nothing."

After we ate, I gently placed Pug on the front seat of the truck. She quickly fell asleep, and soon afterwards I did as well. We peacefully slept next to each other as Rob drove us back home to the comforts of modern civilization.

Rainbow Bridge

Author Unknown

Just this side of heaven is a place called Rainbow Bridge. When an animal dies who has been especially close to someone here, that pet goes to Rainbow Bridge. There are meadows and hills for all of our special friends so they can run and play together. There is plenty of food and water, and sunshine, and our friends are warm and comfortable.

All the animals who have been ill or old are restored to health and vigor; those who were hurt or maimed are made whole and strong again, just as we remember them in our dreams of days and time gone by. The animals are happy and content, except for one small thing; each one misses someone very special who has been left behind.

They all run and play together, but the day comes when one suddenly stops and looks into the distance. His bright eyes are intent; his eager body begins to quiver. All at once he begins to run from the group, flying over the green grass, his legs carrying him faster and faster.

You have been spotted, and when you and your special friend finally meet, you cling together in joyous reunion, never to be parted again. The happy kisses rain upon your face; your hands again caress the beloved head, and you look once more into the trusting eyes of your pet, so long gone from your life but never absent from your heart.

Then you cross Rainbow Bridge together…

Simple Things

by Alan Cunningham

When did I last hold you
Or did I let time slip away.
And isn't it the simple things
That make life beautiful day by day.

"In Memory of Pug August 21, 1991 to August 11, 2002"

My Prayer to You

by Alan Cunningham

Oh, oh, oh, oh, oh
Sing it softly
Oh, oh, oh, oh, oh
Tell it gently
Oh, oh, oh, oh, oh
Write it boldly
Oh, oh, oh, oh, oh
Give it freely

You are the one
You make me happy
You are the one
You make life worthy
You are the one
You give me courage
You are the one
You give life reason

You, oh, oh, oh, oh
You are my love
You, oh, oh, oh, oh
I will miss you
You, oh, oh, oh, oh
Sing it softly
You, oh, oh, oh, oh
Tell it gently

You

About the Author

The Deseret News (Salt Lake City, UT) Utahn hog wild about patients
by Doug Robinson June 3, 2003

Dr. Alan Cunningham has treated both people and animals during his professional career, but if he had to choose one over the other he says he'd probably choose animals. Which would explain the roommates. And the books. And the causes.

A lifelong bachelor, he shares his bed with four dogs he took in after saving their lives. He also has 18 cats, three more dogs, a wild turkey, four peacocks, chickens, doves and geese all crammed into his home and yard in an American Fork neighborhood.

"If something needs a home, I'll provide it," he says, adding, "It's not sitting too well with some of my neighbors."If there was ever a guy whose heart turns to mush every time he sees an animal in pain, it's this guy. When his beloved dog Pug died last year, he wrote a book about it –"Sleeping with Angels." That generated an outpouring of stories from other people whose animals had died, which led to a second book – "On Angels' Wings," a recently released collection of short stories from veterinarians and bereaved pet owners about their own experiences with the loss of an animal friend.

This is how passionate he was about the project: He spent more than $40,000 of his own money to publish, illustrate and distribute the books.

Cunningham wanted to be a veterinarian since he was a kid, so he went to vet school out of college and found he couldn't cut it. He became a respiratory therapist instead; meanwhile, shortly after his 30th birthday he gave vet school another chance, and this time he graduated. He has been a vet for a dozen years, currently working the night shift at an emergency clinic.

In his free time, he is trying to get recognition for war service dogs. He wrote to Gov. Mike Leavitt asking that service animals be honored; the governor agreed and declared that the recent Memorial Day "also be set aside to remember and honor our fallen service animal heroes in Utah."

Cunningham is also writing congressmen hoping to win approval for a postage stamp in honor of service animals, and to create a memorial in Washington, D.C., honoring Vietnam war dogs."More than 4,000 dogs served in Vietnam," he says. "Less than 200 came home. At the end of the war, they were considered equipment and were left behind or euthanized. A lot of the dog handlers wanted to bring them home – they owed their lives to the dogs. These dogs were used to smell out booby traps on the front line – they could hear the wind moving past the guide wires. The Viet Cong would go underwater and breathe through reeds to make a sneak attack; the dogs could smell their breath and alert our soldiers. And basically they were all euthanized."

Most of Cunningham's efforts in behalf of animals take place in the emergency room, where he treats victims of poisonings, fights, seizures, you name it. As you might guess, he is prone to getting attached to his patients. One of them was Aspen, a black lab who was left at the clinic to die – "another one where my heart melted," he says. "We amputated a leg. When she woke up, she looked at me and wagged her tail and I said, 'You're coming home with me.'"

Then there was Angel, a Shih Tzu pup who showed up at the clinic the day after Christmas, half blind and in chronic pain. The owners left her with the clinic. Cunningham took her home and gave her round-the-clock attention for spinal meningitis and nursed her back to health. He sees plenty of sadness in his job; with the loss of a pet, he's seen owners cry, faint and even become suicidal."

For some people, that's all they have are their pets," he says. "Other people don't understand them. They say, 'It's just an animal.' But these are their good friends. My heart breaks. People come in for euthanasia and they're bawling. I try to stay professional, then I leave and shut myself in my room for a while."

Cunningham recently became one of 20 veterinarians awarded a scholarship to (human) medical school as part of an international program using doctors with a background in animal diseases to treat human patients in third-world countries."

I couldn't pass it up," he says. "I'll do both – I'll always be a vet."

Used by permission

Dr. Alan B. Cunningham graduated from Brigham Young University with a Bachelor of Science in Animal Science and a Masters Degree in Respiratory Health Care Science. He also graduated from Utah State University with a PhD in physiology and later from Oregon State University with a Doctorate in Veterinary Medicine. He recently completed his final year in medical school at the University of Health Sciences Antigua.

Dr. Cunningham is the author of four books, including: Sleeping With Angels: A Veterinarian's

Sacred Bond of Animal Companionship. On Angels Wings: Personal Stories About the Passing Away of Beloved Animal Companions. Small Wonders: A Personal Journey to the Wonders of the World. On Angels Wings II: Personal Stories About the Passing Away of Beloved Animal Companions.

Currently he works as a veterinarian at a nighttime emergency clinic. He also volunteers and heads the Utah pet loss hotline as a certified pet loss grief counselor. In addition he volunteers as an advocate for "end of life choices" for humans. He is the recipient of Best of State Utah 2004 for his work as a veterinarian in pet loss and grief support.

Furthermore, he actively campaigns for a commemorative postage stamp and national war memorial for the War Dogs in Vietnam. These valiant warriors gave their lives to save American Soldiers. Nearly 4,000 canine soldiers fought in Vietnam but less than 200 returned stateside. Most were left behind to an uncertain future with the South Vietnamese or euthanized. Many of the dog handlers requested to bring them home because they owed their lives to their canine soldier counterparts. Unfortunately, they were denied. These soldiers desperately want to pay tribute to the War Dogs of Vietnam with commemorative postage stamps and memorials. The postmaster general has denied this request twice and presently a third push is on for a commemorative war dog stamp. Dr. Cunningham urges citizens to write their congressman in behalf of these heroic canine soldiers.

Dr. Cunningham is a lifelong resident of American Fork, Utah.
alancpug2002@yahoo.com

The greatness of a nation and its moral progress
can be judged by the way its animals are treated.
Mahatma Gandhi 1869 – 1948

The soul would have no rainbow had the eye no tear.
Author Unknown

"To every thing there is a season, and
a time to every purpose under the heaven:
A time to be born, and a time to die. . .
A time to weep, and a time to laugh. . .
A time to keep silence, and a time to speak. . .

Ecclesiastes 3:1–7

Pet Loss Support Hotlines

Offered by the American Veterinary Medical Association
http://www.avma.org

(530)752-3602, or toll free (800)565-1526 Staffed by University of California-Davis veterinary students; weekdays, 6:30 pm to 9:30 pm, Pacific Time (PT); http://www.vetmed.ucdavis.edu/petloss/index.htm

(352)392-4700; then dial 1 and 4080, staffed by Florida community volunteers; weekdays, 7 pm to 9 pm, Eastern Time (ET); or call (352)392-4700 X4744 (Joy Diaz) at the University; http://www.vetmed.ufl.edu/vmth/companions.htm

(517)432-2696 Staffed by Michigan State University veterinary students; Tuesday to Thursday, 6:30 pm to 9:30 pm, ET; http://cvm.msu.edu/petloss/index.htm

(630)325-1600 Staffed by Chicago VMA veterinarians and staffs. Leave voice-mail message; calls will be returned 7 pm to 9 pm, CT (Long-distance calls will be returned collect)

(540)231-8038 Staffed by Virginia-Maryland Regional College of Veterinary Medicine; Tuesday, Thursday, 6pm to 9 pm, ET

(614)292-1823 Staffed by The Ohio State University veterinary students; Monday, Wednesday, Friday, 6:30 pm to 9:30 pm, ET; voice-mail messages will be returned, collect, during operating hours

(508)839-7966 Staffed by Tufts University veterinary students; Monday through Friday, 6 pm to 9 pm, ET; voice-mail messages will be returned daily, collect outside Massachusetts; http://www.tufts.edu/vet/petloss/

(888)ISU-PLSH (888-478-7574) Pet Loss Support Hotline hosted by the Iowa State University College of Veterinary Medicine. http://www.vetmed.iastate.edu/animals/petloss/; operational seven days a week, 6pm to 9pm (CST) from Sept-April; Monday, Wednesday, Friday from 6:00-9:00 pm (CST) from May–August.

(607)253-3932 Cornell University Pet Loss Support Hotline staffed by Cornell University Veterinary Students Tuesday–Thursday 6-9pmET, messages will be returned. http://web.vet.cornell.edu/public/petloss/

(217)244-2273 or toll-free (877)394-2273(CARE) Staffed by University of Illinois veterinary students. Sunday, Tuesday and Thursday evenings 7-9 pm Central Time; http://www.cvm.uiuc.edu/CARE/

Argus Institute: Grief Resources, Colorado State University. For the Argus Institute office call (970) 491-4143

(509) 335-5704, Pet Loss Hotline, Washington State University, College of Veterinary Medicine http://www.vetmed.wsu.edu/plhl/index.htm; staffed during the semester on Monday, Tuesday, Wednesday, and Thursday 6:30 — 9:00 PM, and Saturday 1:00–3:00 PM Pacific Time.

(801) 572-HELP (4357) & (801) 756-2640, Dr. Alan B. Cunningham, author on pet loss and grief support, certified pet loss grief counselor, veterinarian, and medical doctor. http://www.petangelsutah.com
e-mail: alancpug2002@yahoo.com

Fragile Tears CD

1. "Fragile Tears" by Gary Stoddard, narrator Alan Cunningham
2. "I Am One Voice" by Gary Stoddard, lead singer Cassidy Toyn
3. "Sunshine After the Rain" by Gary Stoddard, singer Gary Stoddard
4. "Romance Without Words" (Bois Soltare) by Felix Gode Froid, Cathy Clayton–harp
5. "Now I Hold You in My Heart" by Jacki Barineau, lead singer Jacki Barineau
6. "Long Dusty Road" by Judy Reimschiissel, lead singer Judy Reimschiissel
7. "A Hundred Years From Now" by Arthur Gottschalk, Thomas Bacon–horn, Brian Connelly–piano
8. "Simple Things" by Gary Stoddard and Alan Cunningham, singer Phil Miller
9. "Just a Minute" by Diane Hunter, singer Jennifer Dimick
10. "Danza de la Pastora 'Sonatina'" by Ernesto Halffter, Cathy Clayton–harp
11. "Cycle Song of Life (The River Song)" by James Durst, lead singer James Durst
12. "Learning to Love Yourself" by Gary Stoddard, singer Sarah Tucker
13. "My Prayer to You" by Gary Stoddard and Alan Cunningham, lead singer Alan Cunningham